"Christians are pressed by very real questions. How does Scripture structure a church, order worship, organize ministry, and define biblical leadership? Those are just examples of the questions that are answered clearly, carefully, and winsomely in this new series from 9Marks. I am so thankful for this ministry and for its incredibly healthy and hopeful influence in so many faithful churches. I eagerly commend this series."

R. Albert Mohler Jr., President, The Southern Baptist Theological Seminary

"Sincere questions deserve thoughtful answers. If you're not sure where to start in answering these questions, let this series serve as a diving board into the pool. These minibooks are winsomely to-the-point and great to read together with one friend or one hundred friends."

Gloria Furman, author, *Missional Motherhood* and *The Pastor's Wife*

"As a pastor, I get asked lots of questions. I'm approached by unbelievers seeking to understand the gospel, new believers unsure about next steps, and maturing believers wanting help answering questions from their Christian family, friends, neighbors, or coworkers. It's in these moments that I wish I had a book to give them that was brief, answered their questions, and pointed them in the right direction for further study. Church Questions is a series that provides just that. Each booklet tackles one question in a biblical, brief, and practical manner. The series may be called Church Questions, but it could be called 'Church Answers.' I intend to pick these up by the dozens and give them away regularly. You should too."

Juan R. Sanchez, Senior Pastor, High Pointe Baptist Church, Austin, Texas

"Where can we Christians find reliable answers to our common questions about life together at church—without having to plow through long, expensive books? The Church Questions booklets meet our need with answers that are biblical, thoughtful, and practical. For pastors, this series will prove a trustworthy resource for guiding church members toward deeper wisdom and stronger unity."

Ray Ortlund, President, Renewal Ministries

How Can
I Grow in
Hospitality?

Church Questions

How Can
I Grow in
Hospitality?

Keri Folmar

CROSSWAY®

WHEATON, ILLINOIS

Trade paperback ISBN: 978-1-4335-9201-0
ePub ISBN: 978-1-4335-9203-4
PDF ISBN: 978-1-4335-9202-7

Library of Congress Cataloging-in-Publication Data

Names: Folmar, Keri, author.
Title: How can I grow in hospitality? / Keri Folmar.
Description: Wheaton, Illinois : Crossway, 2024. | Series: Church questions | Includes bibliographical references and index.
Identifiers: LCCN 2023030680 (print) | LCCN 2023030681 (ebook) | ISBN 9781433592010 (trade paperback) | ISBN 9781433592027 (pdf) | ISBN 9781433592034 (epub)
Subjects: LCSH: Hospitality—Religious aspects—Christianity. | Church work with new church members. | Christian life—Biblical teaching.
Classification: LCC BV4647.H67 F65 2024 (print) | LCC BV4647.H67 (ebook) | DDC 241/.671—dc23/eng/20240216
LC record available at https://lccn.loc.gov/2023030680
LC ebook record available at https://lccn.loc.gov/2023030681

Crossway is a publishing ministry of Good News Publishers.

BP		33	32	31	30	29	28	27	26	25	24
15	14	13	12	11	10	9	8	7	6	5	4	3	2	1

And they devoted themselves to the apostles' teaching and the fellowship, to the breaking of bread and the prayers. And awe came upon every soul, and many wonders and signs were being done through the apostles. And all who believed were together and had all things in common. And they were selling their possessions and belongings and distributing the proceeds to all, as any had need. And day by day, attending the temple together and breaking bread in their homes, they received their food with glad and generous hearts.

Acts 2:42–46

Hospitality isn't one of my strengths. My family has had many opportunities to welcome people into our home in Dubai, but we haven't always been great hosts. We've definitely made our share of hospitality faux pas.

One November, an esteemed theologian was with us for a week of teaching, and I forgot to turn on the hot water heater in his bathroom. When I realized what had happened I asked if his shower was cold. "It was brisk," he politely responded.

Another time, a couple of pastors from our previous church came to visit. They had a meeting at our church that went late into the night. When they got back to our villa, they found the doors locked. My husband, according to his normal routine, had secured all the locks before we went to bed. The two men ended up sleeping in front of the house in a compact car. That same trip our water pump broke, and we couldn't offer them water in the morning. I wonder why they haven't been back to visit?

But wait, there's more! We've run out of food while hosting large groups from our church. I've cooked meals our guests haven't liked. I've also done some things that could have been downright offensive to our guests. When our Muslim friend, Reem, came over for lunch, we accidentally set out the placemats that showed a picture of a pig on a French country farm.[1] Some Muslims will not even eat in a home where they suspect pork has been consumed. The whole point of our meal was to share the gospel not offend our guest! Thankfully, Reem was a good sport and laughed it off.

So I'm admitting up front that I'm not the queen of hospitality. In fact, I'm hospitality-challenged. I don't spend a lot of time decorating my house. Worn-out furniture in the Folmar Villa gets covered with blankets rather than replaced. I'm not an extrovert either. I'm almost always a little stressed when preparing to have people over. I don't even enjoy cooking; and baking is definitely out, as I don't eat sugar or flour.

But despite all these setbacks, I have grown in my love for hospitality. Hospitality has been graciously extended to me by other Christians, and I've learned it's an indispensable way to serve the body of Christ.

Biblical hospitality is the practice of welcoming others into our lives. Hospitality means inviting someone to share a meal, shelter, or a ride, so you can get to know each other on a deeper level. Hospitality entails providing an environment of care for our brothers and sisters in Christ or for the stranger with whom we want to share Christ. Hospitality means gladly receiving the neighbor next door or the traveling saint in need of refreshment.

Hospitality in the church is ultimately rooted in God's hospitality toward us. From the first pages of Genesis, God created a place for his people—a place where he would share his life with them. He literally breathed his life into Adam and Eve and put them in a beautiful garden with every tree that was "pleasant to the sight and good for food" (Gen. 2:9). Imagine that lavish hospitality! In the garden, God dwelled with his people, welcoming them into his presence.

But Adam and Eve eventually turned away God's hospitality. They wanted to provide for themselves and ate from the only tree God had prohibited.

Yet even after his people rejected him, God still showed hospitality to sinners. He clothed them and cared for them. Although they had been expelled from the garden and would now eat bread only "by the sweat of [their] face" (Gen. 3:19), God gave them animal skins for cover, and every bit of the bread for which they toiled was ultimately provided by his hand.

God's hospitality toward sinners continues as a major feature in the stories of the Old

Testament. God sustained Israel with water and manna in the wilderness (Deut. 8:2–3) and welcomed them into the promised land— a bountiful land flowing with milk and honey (Joshua 5–6). He caused vines to shade disobedient prophets (Jonah 4:6), and sheltered exiled kings in caves where they could hide from enemies (1 Samuel 24).

Finally, in his greatest act of hospitality, God sent his Son to welcome his enemies to his table. The bread of life came into the world and said, "Whoever comes to me shall not hunger, and whoever believes in me shall never thirst" (John 6:35). Jesus, the Prince of heaven, "came not to be served but to serve, and to give his life as a ransom for many" (Mark 10:45).

Our sin left us spiritually naked, homeless, and starving. In the death of Jesus, God offers us clothing to cover our shame, shelter for refuge, and a meal that will fill us with the fullness of eternal life. In Christ, God welcomes us into his family. Not surprisingly, the symbol of Christ's death instituted by our Lord is itself a meal. One with Christ and united to one another in the church, we eat and drink in remembrance of the price he paid to ransom us to God. The broken bread and poured-out wine, a picture of Christ's body and blood, remind us of God's hospitality toward us and beckon us to show hospitality to one another.

God extends hospitality in the gospel. So we who believe the gospel imitate his hospitality. As God welcomes us, we welcome others. We see this happen all over the Bible. When Zacchaeus met Jesus, his immediate response was to "joyfully" take Jesus into his home (Luke 19:6), and when Lydia's heart was opened she urged Paul and his cohort to come stay at her house (Acts 16:14–15). Believers want to welcome Christ and each other into their lives.

Hospitality isn't just our hearts' response to the gospel, God also commands us to be hospitable. In Romans 12, Paul appeals to the saints to present their bodies to God as living sacrifices (12:1). What does that look like? "Contribut[ing] to the needs of the saints and seek[ing] to show hospitality" (12:13).

In Hebrews, the command to show hospitality to strangers also follows the command to offer acceptable worship to God: "Do not neglect to show hospitality to strangers, for thereby some have entertained angels unawares" (Heb. 13:2).

In 1 Peter 4, the apostle warns of the coming judgment, writing, "The end of all things is at hand" (4:7). In light of that coming final day, Peter encourages the saints to "show hospitality to one another without grumbling" (4:9).

From these verses, we see that hospitality is an act of worship. It is an expression of love to God and to others. Hospitality, then, is an intentional expression of genuine sacrificial love to a brother or sister in Christ. Hospitality isn't merely providing food and a bed. It's pointing another image-bearer godward by welcoming that person into our lives and hearts for the sake of Christ. True hospitality is the open-handed acknowledgment of the goodness of God toward us that overflows to others.

Do you see your hospitality as a sacrifice of love for God and for others?

Now maybe you're ready to make this kind of sacrifice, but you keep getting tripped up by your worn-out couch and chipped wall paint. Maybe you're calculating how much money is left in your bank account this month and aren't sure you can feed yourself, let alone others. Does a lump rise to your throat as you wonder how you will juggle supervising the kids while cooking and still be able to engage in conversation when the guests arrive? Or maybe you're a young single man and wonder how you could possibly invite a family over and feed them a meal.

Let's see if I can alleviate some of your anxieties. Here are eight ways you can grow in your love for and practice of hospitality no matter who you are:

1. Grow in Love for the Church

Hospitality is an expression of earnest, genuine love. So it follows that we will grow in hospitality *in* the church as we grow in love *for* the church. Actually the arrow points both ways. Love increases our hospitality, and hospitality increases our love.

Two women in our church are a perfect example. Adiam is from Eritrea. Nanette is from the Philippines. The two couldn't be more different, but they have Christ and their local church in common. Adiam started giving Nanette rides to church. Rides turned into long conversations, which turned into meals and family affairs. Now Adiam's family includes Nanette in all their gatherings, and she is beloved by Adiam's ninety-year-old mother. Here's the shocking thing: Adiam's mom knows Nanette's love without words. They can't even speak the same language. Anyone looking from the outside would be perplexed about Adiam and Nanette's relationship. But Christ and his church ties together the most unlikely of people.

In John 13, Jesus tells his disciples, "A new commandment I give to you, that you love one another: just as I have loved you, you also are to love one another. By this all people will know that you are my disciples, if you have love for one another" (John 13:34–35).

Why does Jesus call this "a new commandment"? God has already told his people to love their neighbors in Leviticus 19:18. What's different now?

First, Christ provides an elevated standard for love. Christians are to love each other the way Jesus has loved us—radical, self-sacrificing, undeserving love! Jesus gives his disciples this new commandment just after washing their feet. Only the lowest of servants washed the feet of their masters, and yet the Savior washes their feet and tells them to do the same to one another (John 13:14–15). The washing of feet was a picture for the disciples of what Jesus would do on the cross (Matt. 20:28). Later, Jesus says, "Greater love has no one than this, that someone lay down his life for his friends" (John 15:13). Jesus laid down his life for us so that we would lay down our lives for one another. That is the standard of Christian love (1 John 4:11).

Second, this commandment is "new" because Christians are under a new covenant— they are "a chosen race, a royal priesthood, a holy nation, a people for [God's] own possession" (1 Pet. 2:9). Unlike members of the old covenant, they don't just possess the law but they also possess the Spirit, enabling sacrificial acts of love. Their commission is to "proclaim the excellencies of him who called [them] out of darkness into his marvelous light" (2:9). As they proclaim Christ's excellencies, outsiders will observe their love for one another and see the great worth of Christ. Their love can't be explained in any other way.

We are to show God's love for those inside the church and proclaim his excellencies to those outside. That's why when you exercise hospitality in the church, you should make a practice to invite unbelievers. We want them to notice a difference in us.

My family recently hosted a visitor from out of town. We made it our aim to simply include him in the normal routine of our lives. We brought him along as a Moroccan couple hosted us for dinner. He joined us for another meal with a small group of church members. We shared testimonies of salvation and of God's goodness in our lives. Our visitor was blown away. He later told my husband how affected he was by the hospitality in the life of our church. Our dinner parties included empty nesters, widows, young couples with toddlers, and a few singles. There is no way apart from Christ to explain the deep love for one another that was expressed at those dinners. We have nothing but Christ in common.

In your church, when you spend time together sharing what the Lord has done, loving one another as Christ has loved you, you will affect those on the outside and draw them in.

Coworkers, neighbors, parents from your children's school, people at the gym: you may have a lot in common with them. But with whom does your heart long to spend time? Who refreshes and encourages you most?

The more you love your church, the more you will want to know her members. The better you know the members, the more you'll love them.

In other words, hospitality increases your love for your church. Increased love for your church simultaneously increases your hospitality.

TIP

Ask questions to encourage meaningful conversations among your guests, such as:

- *"What did you think of the second point in the sermon?"*
- *"What have you been reading lately?"*
- *"I noticed how intentional you are with Joe. How have you cultivated that kind of compassion?"*
- *"How have you seen God's goodness in the last week?"*

2. Welcome Widely

In Romans 15:7, Paul writes: "Therefore welcome one another as Christ has welcomed you, for the glory of God." There are many ways to welcome one another into our lives and hearts. It all starts with the weekly church gathering. At corporate worship we get to forget about ourselves and warmly welcome one another with a hearty handshake, hug, or kiss.

My friend Elizabeth is great at this. She is so excited every time we see each other that

I feel her love from the expression on her face. One time we were talking with my kids about shyness, and Elizabeth told us her simple secret: when she walks into a gathering, she looks for people to encourage. She joyfully greets them and asks them questions about their lives. She forgets how she's coming off and makes it about them. I often remember Elizabeth's goal to build up others when I walk into a situation feeling insecure. Christian, get to church early and extend a warm welcome to your brothers and sisters in Christ.

We can extend this welcome throughout corporate worship. For instance, congregational singing is an act of hospitality. We welcome each other by singing heartily to one another. In that moment we are worshiping God and encouraging one another. Keep your eyes, ears, and mouth open, and look at your brothers and sisters as they lift up their voices to the Lord. Spur others on in worship with an exuberant voice and let them spur you on. "Be filled with the Spirit, addressing one another in psalms and hymns and spiritual songs, singing and making melody to the Lord with your heart" (Eph. 5:18–19).

We also welcome one another with heartfelt corporate readings and audible "amens" in response to corporate prayers. And we welcome one another as we speak God's word to each other, letting "the word of Christ dwell in [us] richly, teaching and admonishing one another in all wisdom" (Col. 3:16). Listen intently to the preaching and talk about it with others before you leave. Start your hospitality during the weekly gathering and then let it continue throughout the week. Before the Lord's Day ends, perhaps have someone over for lunch or organize a gathering at the park.

Also remember, you can exercise hospitality in a number of different ways in addition to having people in your home. Take another member of your church out for lunch during the week. Give someone a ride to church or Bible study. Grab coffee with a friend. Visit an elderly member in a nursing home. Host a game or movie night. If you're married, invite singles over. If you're single, invite families. If you're an introvert, invite another introvert. If you're an extrovert, throw a party!

The point is, there are many ways to practice hospitality. Team up with others or do it alone. Open your home or invite someone out. Take a meal to a new mom or a struggling saint. Or let someone bring a meal to you when you're going through a difficult time.

Hospitality is not just a practice for housewives with large homes. It's not just for women (have you ever noticed that being hospitable is a qualification for pastors?). All Christians—men, women, students, parents, singles—are called to exercise hospitality.

Be strategic. Open your heart and welcome your brothers and sisters into your life for the glory of God, "just as Christ has welcomed you" (Rom. 15:7).

TIP

For lunch after church, throw meat and vegetables into a Crock-Pot in the morning with a few cloves of garlic and an onion, flavored with salt and pepper and any other favorite spices you enjoy. Add a little broth or water and let it cook on high. Measure water and rice into a rice cooker or pot. Flip that on as soon as you get home and have fruit on hand for dessert. You've got a hearty, no-fuss meal ready to serve.

3. Don't Neglect the Main Course

As we show hospitality, we need to keep the main thing the main thing—loving Christ ourselves and helping others do the same. Think about Mary and Martha, the two sisters whom Jesus visited in Luke 10. Martha was upset at her sister for being lazy and inconsiderate, just sitting there at Jesus's feet while Martha was working hard to serve everyone. Martha got annoyed and told Jesus to make Mary get up and help!

But Jesus didn't rebuke Mary for her lack of hospitality. He rebuked Martha. How many times the Lord could have said the same thing to me: Keri, Keri, "you are anxious and troubled about many things, but one thing is necessary" (Luke 10:41–42). That one thing is learning from Jesus; communing with him—that is the good portion that will not be taken away. Martha missed the importance of keeping Christ at the center of her affections, even as she "welcomed [Jesus] into her house" (10:38). Sometimes I miss it too. I get caught up in what I'm doing and forget who I'm doing it with and doing it for.

When we welcome people into our homes, cars, or local cafés, we need to keep the main thing the main thing. Practice hospitality for the sake of pointing others to Jesus. Hospitality that doesn't focus on building relationships and pointing others to Christ is like serving a meal without the main course.

Have you ever been to someone's house only to find the hosts so busy in the kitchen or so focused on their kids that you were unable to have a conversation with your host or hostess? I've been there as a guest; it can make you feel uncomfortable, even invisible. I've also been there as a hostess. I found that simplifying our meals and putting on a video for the kids after dinner frees us up to have focused, meaningful conversations with our guests. If you have little ones, get advice and ideas from other parents about how to shepherd your children while also having guests in your home. You might want to invite another family in the same stage of life, so the kids can play together, or you may need to schedule coffee at naptime or dessert after the kids are in bed. Also consider ways you can include your kids in hospitality. Involve them in game nights or help them make dessert for your guests.

Of course, there will be times when all our plans go awry. But instead of hiding in another room or giving up, we can admit our weakness and ask for help. Then our guests know we're not superhuman. One way to love our guests is by showing them that we're weak sinners just like they are by welcoming them into our mess.

One quick caveat: remember you don't have to do this alone. Just because you're the host doesn't mean you have to be responsible to lead every conversation. Sometimes just opening your home and letting other Christians care for one another is all you need to do. Your hospitality can become a platform for the caring, relational work of other brothers and sisters.

Whether you're a mom with young children, a student with a lot of studying to do, or a businessman with an intense career, organize your hospitality in a way that enables you to focus on relationships and building others up in Christ.

TIP

If you have children or are hosting a group, invite a young single person or two from your church into your family to host with you. They can help you juggle your guests and children, and you can train them practically in hospitality—you might even learn a thing or two about hospitality from them as well!

4. Aim to Bless, Not Impress

Fine china or paper plates? Gourmet or Instapot? Leather furniture or folding chairs? What is your aim in hospitality? If I notice I'm feeling particularly stressed when having others into our home, I know I need to pause to examine my heart. Am I doing it for the good of the church and ultimately for the glory of Christ or for my own reputation? Am I working in a flurry so that things look perfect when people walk in the door, or am I working hard so I can sit down and engage with my guests when they arrive? Have I prayed for those who are coming over, or have I put God on the shelf only to be taken back down when we ask him to bless the meal?

Hospitality is not about how we look but how we make Christ look. Even in hospitality we need to remember that we have died, and it is Christ who lives in us (Gal. 2:20). So we should engage in the work of hospitality ultimately out of devotion to Christ and in obedience to his word. The aim of our hospitality is love for God and love for the people of God. Galatians 6:10 says: "Let us do good to everyone, and especially to those who are of the household of faith."

Of course, someone who is good at decorating or bakes delicious treats can bless others with those talents. But we want to do those things out of love in our hearts not out of pressure to impress. We do no good to others by impressing them. In fact, aiming to impress can make others feel inadequate.

On one occasion I had lunch with some wives whose husbands were heading into the pastorate, and they sheepishly expressed their fear about being pastors' wives. After some digging, I got to the root of the problem: they were afraid they couldn't handle the hospitality that would be required of them. I was confused. These women had warm personalities, and they were excited about their husbands' ministries. I probed a little deeper, asking them what they thought would be expected of them. They described spending long days in the kitchen cooking full meals for anyone who wanted to come over. One confessed that she would be miserable spending that much time in the kitchen (me too!), and the other said her family would never be able to afford the groceries.

It turns out all of them had been observing one particular extroverted woman in the church, whose greatest joy was cooking, as the model for biblical hospitality. She loved chatting with others in her kitchen while her husband entertained the rest of the guests. These women had lost the plot, seeing this woman's gifts as the *only way* to be hospitable. They started to focus more on how they could impress as she did, rather than on how they could bless.

Let me assure you, whether you're an introvert or extrovert, if you aim to bless and not impress, hospitality will be doable for you. Figure out simple meals. Have your guests bring a dish. Use paper plates. People want to know you, not have a fine dining experience.

One of Jesus's most amazing miracles was an act of supernatural hospitality—feeding a meal to over five thousand men, women, and children (John 6). But go back and read that story again. You'll find Jesus didn't want people to focus on the food. He wanted the focus on him and his teaching (6:35).

When we try to impress through our hospitality, we end up putting the spotlight on ourselves. Instead our aim should be to spotlight

Jesus and to love others. Christ is magnified *by* our love for one another. He's glorified in our cooking or decorating, not by the tastiness or beauty, but as we use them to focus on him! This is how we aim to bless.

> *Use paper plates and cups (or individual bottles and cans) to cut way back on the cleanup when you have people over for a meal in your home.*

5. Imitate but Don't Envy

After telling the church in Corinth to "do all to the glory of God" (1 Cor. 10:31), Paul tells them to imitate him, as he imitates Christ (1 Cor. 11:1). Human beings are imitators. Think of a baby's first words. His mother and father keep saying, "Mama!" and "Dada!" and to their delight, he soon mimics their words. Even a baby's hand gestures and facial expressions are often learned behaviors—so be careful what you roll your eyes at! Imitation is natural for humans; it's how we learn.

When you witness others practicing hospitality, imitate what you like and what works for your life. Do they have a way of arranging their living room that facilitates conversation? How do they serve drinks or food in a convenient way that would make things easier for you? What sort of easy-to-make meals do they serve that might make hospitality more doable for you?

My husband, John, and I had the privilege of staying with our friends Aaron and Deana for an extended period of time during a sabbatical. They did heaps of hospitality during our visit. We felt so welcome in their home that it inspired us to welcome more people into our home.

During our time with them, we saw several things we wanted to replicate in our own lives. For example: (1) Aaron intentionally questioned people around the dinner table. (2) Deana didn't just *text* women but *called* them to find out how they were doing. (3) They asked a dozen church members to grab takeout and bring it over to their house for fellowship after the Sunday evening prayer gathering.

At the same time, while it's helpful to learn from and be inspired by other members, we need to make sure that as we observe our brothers and sisters, we don't become envious of their gifts and abilities. Churches are made up of a diversity of people, together displaying the manifold wisdom of God (Eph. 3:10). Your church needs members with a variety of gifts and from all kinds of cultures and socio-economic backgrounds. Some of our sisters and brothers might live in big, beautiful homes. Others might love to cook gourmet meals and know how to serve them with style. Some might be naturally charismatic and sociable. Some might be introverts, particularly gifted with one-on-one conversations rather than entertaining a crowd. We won't have the ability to imitate everything others do. But don't let that reality serve as an occasion for envy or sinful comparison. Instead, praise the Creator who made us all with such unique gifts.

I had two friends from very different backgrounds. One was married to a top executive, and the other worked at an office. They were both very social and were good friends with each other. The wealthier woman had a beautiful villa and did lots of hospitality both to support her husband and bless the church. She was a friend to many types of people. She hosted other top executives as well as members from our church who lived in labor camps. But each time the less affluent woman entered her house, she saw the life she wanted to live. She began to feel that she wasn't getting her fair share and eventually was so eaten up with bitterness that she blew up the relationship and left the church.

Our envy of others might not rise to that level, but we need to check our hearts. The Bible lists envy alongside malice, deceit, hypocrisy, slander, and even murder (Rom. 1:29; 1 Pet. 2:1). It was envy that led Jewish leaders to crucify Christ (Matt. 27:18)! Also, let me say from years of discipling in the church, I think hospitality-envy is a particular issue for women. It's easy to compare ourselves with other sisters. We're often tempted to think, *Her meals are tastier than mine. Her house is better decorated.* And on it goes.

Brother or sister, if you're comparing his chili or her guest bathroom to yours, beware. Galatians 5:26 warns, "Let us not become conceited, provoking one another, envying one another." Competitiveness has no place in the church. Imitate the good, but don't envy what God has given to others. Hasn't he been abundantly good to you?

TIP

When you have guests coming over, budget your time and make lists: groceries, cooking, cleaning. Do your best to get items checked off ahead of time, so you can focus on your guests during their visit.

6. Extend Hospitality beyond Your Church

The New Testament word translated as hospitality is literally "love of strangers." We know we're not wrong in applying the term to welcoming those in our churches because each of the hospitality commands is nestled within passages about brotherly love. At the same time, while our hospitality should *start* in our local churches, it shouldn't *stop* there. In addition to welcoming one another, we should welcome unbelievers, as well as needy saints.

Once when Jesus dined in the house of a Pharisee, he said to his host:

> When you give a dinner or a banquet, do not invite your friends or your brothers or your relatives or rich neighbors, lest they also invite you in return and you be repaid. But when you give a feast, invite the poor, the crippled, the lame, the blind, and you will be blessed, because they cannot repay you. For you will be repaid at the resurrection of the just. (Luke 14:12–14)

The world schemes and calculates, "What can I get out of this in this life?" But Christians are strategically storing up treasure in heaven. Imagine the meals and accommodation there!

We bonded with our former next-door neighbors because they had kids the same age as ours and a friendly labrador who liked to play with our golden retriever. They had lived in Dubai for a long time and were happy to join us for dinner and attend our Christmas carol parties, but they never showed interest in the gospel.

Nevertheless, when a Muslim friend of theirs wanted a Bible, they came to us. As a result, I was able to lead my neighbor and her Muslim friend in a Bible study through the Gospel of Mark. Eventually both started coming to church.

How well do you know your neighbors? I confess, my husband and I have gone through seasons of being more or less involved with our neighbors—often realizing that we had wrongly become too "busy" to reach out. But fellow Christian, make time to invite your unbelieving neighbors into your life for the sake of the gospel.

Remember, you don't have to go it alone. Are there other church members in your neighborhood with whom you can partner? For instance, I know several women who rotate hosting neighbors for dessert. They use "get to know you" questions aimed at deepening their conversations and have found that many neighborhood women are lonely and in need of friends. Through rotating dessert nights, they have ample opportunity to share the best news in the world with their neighbors.

Do you have neighbors, coworkers, friends from school, or other relationships you can invest in for kingdom purposes?

And what about the poor, the crippled, the lame, and the blind? Is there a prison you can visit? A retirement home? A crisis pregnancy center? Is someone in the hospital? Can you invite someone into your home who cannot return the favor? Jesus welcomes those with nothing to give, and so it should also be with us. Thank God that Jesus extends his welcome beyond those of worldly repute—even to the likes of you and me!

TIP

If you don't have kids but want to have families over, ask people for old toys and books or buy used toys at a discount. Then you can welcome children into your home, and when they get bored with adult conversation, they'll have toys to play with and books to read.

Another way of extending hospitality beyond your church is by opening your home to missionaries or traveling saints. Living in Dubai, we've had this kind of welcome offered to us numerous times when we've traveled back to the United States. We've been shown hospitality by longtime friends in Austin, new friends in Williamsburg, a single pastor who bought a big home in Texas to house missionaries on furlough, and other dear saints who have sacrificed their time and space to make us feel welcome. We've even had a family give us their car to drive for months at a time. These saints remind me of Gaius whom John commends in 3 John 5–6:

Beloved, it is a faithful thing you do in all your efforts for these brothers, strangers as they are, who testified to your love before the church. You will do well to send them on their journey in a manner worthy of God.

Gospel-workers depend on the hospitality of the saints.

The book of Acts is a record of hospitality extended in the early church. People like Jason, Priscilla, and Aquila risked their necks to show hospitality to those who were preaching the gospel. Hospitality toward gospel-workers is all over Paul's epistles. He expects hospitality for himself from both churches and individuals (Rom. 15:24, 32; Philem. 22). He asks the churches in Rome to show hospitality to Phoebe, writing, "Welcome her in the Lord in a way worthy of the saints, and help her in whatever she may need from you" (Rom. 16:2). He asks the Colossians to welcome Mark and Titus and to help Zenus and Apollos as they travel through Crete, instructing, "See that they lack nothing" (Titus 3:13).

Housing and supporting traveling missionaries and gospel-workers is a privilege—one that is mutually beneficial. Hearing about what's happening in other parts of the world makes us thankful for our access to Bibles and fellow believers, and it spurs us on to pray for those who haven't yet heard the gospel. One day, we'll worship God face-to-face with the people we've prayed for!

Do you have a spare room or an empty basement? Use them to bless missionaries you know or that your church supports. Who knows? The Lord may just use one visiting missionary to get you overseas for gospel work too.

As God has welcomed us, we have the responsibility and privilege to extend our welcome to others beyond our local church.

TIP

Before overnight guests come into town, ask them what you can have on hand for breakfast and what they like to drink.

Stock up on these things and fill a basket with some snacks. Then you can give them free rein to help themselves in your kitchen.

7. Do the Work of Ministry

Paul includes "hospitable" in the list of the qualifications for pastors, also called elders (1 Tim. 3:2; Titus 1:8). As church members are welcomed into the homes of their pastors and elders, they learn hospitality from their way of life. The hospitality of elders in a church creates a cascading effect in the life of the congregation. Pastors teach the word and show hospitality, members then imitate their pastors and extend that same hospitality to each other. That's the biblical pattern: pastors teach and model, and the saints do the work of ministry (Eph. 4:12–13).

I've witnessed this reality in my own church on countless occasions. I think of John, an elder in our church, and his wife, Lisa, having an open home where a young couple, Jonny and Anna, spent significant time and were discipled. Now Jonny and Anna host a regular "after-party" for young people after our Sunday evening service, ministering to others just as John and Lisa ministered to them.

Hospitality facilitates much of the other ministry Scripture requires of Christians: evangelism, fellowship, care, and teaching. Hospitality is often the platform from which we can build up the body of Christ.

Again, I've seen this repeatedly in my own context. Bethany goes out of her way to invite families over to her apartment for meals. Isaam and Sandra host different families every week after church. Fountain and Rachel always have an open door for saints needing encouragement. Jonathan and Amelie host overnight boating trips with others in our church where they share the gospel with their Muslim captain. Andy rounds up the young people for gatherings at his home or at a restaurant everyone can afford. And on it goes. These brothers and sisters are doing the work of ministry, building up the church.

TIP

Get your kids involved in your hospitality even when they're young. Give them each a task to do the day before you have people over and include them in serving the meal and cleaning up. This will teach them to love others in this way and, eventually (wink wink), they'll be helpful to you.

8. Think of the Reward

Jesus said that on the final day, all the nations will gather before his throne, and he will separate people from one another like a shepherd separates the sheep from the goats.

Then the King will say to those on his right, "Come, you who are blessed by my Father, inherit the kingdom prepared for you from the foundation of the world. For I was hungry and you gave me food, I was thirsty and you gave me drink, I was a stranger and you welcomed me . . ." Then the righteous will answer him, saying, "Lord, when did we see you hungry and feed you, or thirsty and give you drink? And when did we see you a stranger and welcome you, or naked and clothe you?" . . . And the King will answer them, "Truly, I say to you, as you did it to one of the least of these my brothers, you did it to me." (Matt. 25:34–40)

A small act of kindness—food and drink—a great reward! Why is the reward so great? Because by showing hospitality to the King's servants, we show hospitality to the King himself! We don't deserve such reward, but we're given abundantly more than all we can ask or imagine (Eph. 3:20). Surely, we can extend hospitality to welcome others in his precious name.

TIP

For sharing dinner with others on a tight budget try:

- *ramen noodles with eggs*
- *pasta in marinara sauce, spiced with a variety of herbs and some chili flakes*

- *ask guests to bring their own meals with them*
- *host a potluck*

God extended hospitality to us! He welcomed us into the fellowship of his family. Like the father of the prodigal son, his arms were open wide, and he has prepared a banquet for us (Luke 15:11–24).

As Christians, we no longer live for ourselves but for Christ and his people. Sin once separated us from God and each other. But Jesus died and rose again so that our sin could be wiped away. We are now united to Christ our Savior by faith, adopted by the Father, and indwelt by the Holy Spirit. Even more, God has nestled us into local bodies of believers and adopted us into a worldwide family so that, wherever we go, we have brothers and sisters to love. What a privilege!

So "seek to show hospitality" (Rom. 12:13). Don't neglect it (Heb. 13:2). Do it without grumbling (1 Pet. 4:9). And as you do, remember that one day soon the worldwide family of Christ will be joined together, gathered around his throne. No more hospitality will be needed. We'll be his guests at the banquet table of the Lamb (Rev. 19:9).

Note

1. This story (as well as others in this booklet) is shared with permission, and some names have been changed for privacy.

Scripture Index

IX 9Marks

Building Healthy Churches

9Marks exists to equip church leaders with a biblical vision and practical resources for displaying God's glory to the nations through healthy churches.

To that end, we want to see churches characterized by these nine marks of health:

1. Expositional Preaching
2. Gospel Doctrine
3. A Biblical Understanding of Conversion and Evangelism
4. Biblical Church Membership
5. Biblical Church Discipline
6. A Biblical Concern for Discipleship and Growth
7. Biblical Church Leadership
8. A Biblical Understanding of the Practice of Prayer
9. A Biblical Understanding and Practice of Missions

Find all our Crossway titles and other resources at 9Marks.org.

IX 9Marks Church Questions

Providing ordinary Christians with sound and
accessible biblical teaching by answering
common questions about church life.

For more information, visit crossway.org.